The Direct and Unmistaken Method of Purifying Yourself of and Protecting Yourself Against the Causes of Problems

Previously published by the
LAMA YESHE WISDOM ARCHIVE

Becoming Your Own Therapist, by Lama Yeshe
Advice for Monks and Nuns, by Lama Yeshe and Lama Zopa Rinpoche
Virtue and Reality, by Lama Zopa Rinpoche
Make Your Mind an Ocean, by Lama Yeshe
Teachings from the Vajrasattva Retreat, by Lama Zopa Rinpoche
Daily Purification: A Short Vajrasattva Practice, by Lama Zopa Rinpoche
The Essence of Tibetan Buddhism, by Lama Yeshe
Making Life Meaningful, by Lama Zopa Rinpoche
Teachings from the Mani Retreat, by Lama Zopa Rinpoche

FOR INITIATES ONLY

A Chat about Heruka, by Lama Zopa Rinpoche
A Chat about Yamantaka, by Lama Zopa Rinpoche

IN ASSOCIATION WITH TDL PUBLICATIONS, LOS ANGELES

Mirror of Wisdom, by Geshe Tsultim Gyeltsen
Illuminating the Path, by His Holiness the Dalai Lama (forthcoming 2002)

*May whoever sees, touches, reads, remembers, or talks or thinks
about these booklets never be reborn in unfortunate circumstances,
receive only rebirths in situations conducive to the perfect practice of
Dharma, meet only perfectly qualified spiritual guides, quickly
develop bodhicitta and immediately attain enlightenment for the
sake of all sentient beings.*

LAMA ZOPA RINPOCHE

THE DIRECT AND UNMISTAKEN METHOD
of Purifying Yourself of and Protecting Yourself
Against the Causes of Problems such as Cancer, AIDS,
Depression, Difficult Relationships, Earthquakes, Terrorism,
Economic Troubles and so forth, and of
Bringing Happiness to All Beings

THE PRACTICE AND BENEFITS OF THE
EIGHT MAHAYANA PRECEPTS

Commentaries by
Trijang Dorje Chang and Geshe Lamrimpa

Compiled and translated by
Lama Zopa Rinpoche

LAMA YESHE WISDOM ARCHIVE
Boston

www.LamaYeshe.com
A non-profit charitable organization for the benefit of
all sentient beings and a section of the
Foundation for the Preservation of the Mahayana Tradition
www.fpmt.org

First published by Wisdom Publications, 1991
This revised edition published 2002
10,000 copies for free distribution

LAMA YESHE WISDOM ARCHIVE
PO Box 356
Weston
MA 02493 USA

ISBN 1-891868-11-X
10 9 8 7 6 5 4 3 2 1

Cover painting by
Peter Iseli

Cover and book design by
Lisa Sawlit

Please contact the LAMA YESHE WISDOM ARCHIVE for copies
of our free books

Printed in Canada on recycled, acid-free paper

Contents

Benefactor's Dedication

In memory of my beloved parents, Miriam Merlien Slight McWilliams (1914–1983) and Joseph Gleason McWilliams (1923–2001)

In all their future lives, may my parents attain only fortunate rebirths, be guided by kind and holy spiritual masters, and quickly achieve enlightenment for the benefit of all sentient beings.

—Petra

In the joyous mandala of Amitabha Buddha
May I be reborn from a beautiful lotus,
And may I there have the pleasure of gaining
A pure prophecy from Amitabha himself.

Having won this word of prophecy,
By the power of mind may I fill all directions
With many millions of mystical emanations
And bring limitless benefits to the world.

—from the King of Prayers

The publisher thanks Petra McWilliams for sponsoring this book in memory of her late parents.

Publisher's Acknowledgments

We are extremely grateful to our friends and supporters who have made it possible for the LAMA YESHE WISDOM ARCHIVE to both exist and function: to Lama Yeshe and Lama Zopa Rinpoche, whose kindness is impossible to repay; to Peter and Nicole Kedge and Venerable Ailsa Cameron for helping bring the ARCHIVE to its present state of development; to Venerable Roger Kunsang, Lama Zopa's tireless assistant, for his kindness and consideration; and to our sustaining supporters: Drs. Penny Noyce & Leo Liu, Barry & Connie Hershey, Joan Terry, Roger & Claire Ash-Wheeler, Claire Atkins, Richard Gere, Ecie Hursthouse, Lily Chang Wu, T. Y. Alexander, Therese Miller, Chris Dornan, Henry & Catherine Lau, Tom & Suzanne Castles, Datuk Tai Tsu Kuang, Chuah Kok Leng, the Caytons (Lori, Karuna, Pam, Bob & Amy), Tom Thorning, Tan Swee Eng, Salim Lee, Doren & Mary Harper, Claire Ritter, Sandra Magnussen, Cecily Drucker, Lynnea Elkind, Janet Moore, Su Hung, Carol Davies, Jack Morison, Dorian Ribush and Dharmawati Brechbuhl. We also thank most sincerely Massimo Corona and the FPMT International Office for their generous financial and administrative assistance.

We would like, as well, to express our appreciation for the kindness and compassion of all those generous benefactors mentioned in detail in our previous publications. They are too numerous to mention individually in this little book, but we value highly each and every contribution made to spreading the Dharma for the sake of the kind mother sentient beings.

We would also like to thank the many kind people who have asked that their donations be kept anonymous; the volunteers who have given so generously of their time to help us with our mailings, especially Therese Miller; our dedicated office staff, Jennifer Barlow and Angie Gittleman; Alison Ribush & Mandala Books (Melbourne) for much appreciated assistance with our work in Australia; and Dennis Heslop, Philip Bradley and our other friends at Wisdom Books (London) for their great help with our work in Europe.

Finally, we are most grateful to Peter Iseli for so kindly offering us the cover painting and to Lisa Sawlit for so beautifully designing this book.

If you, dear reader, would like to join this noble group of open-hearted altruists by contributing to the production of more free booklets by Lama Yeshe or Lama Zopa Rinpoche or to any other aspect of the LAMA YESHE WISDOM ARCHIVE's work, please contact us to find out how.

—*Dr. Nicholas Ribush*

Through the merit of having contributed to the spread of the Buddha's teachings for the sake of all sentient beings, may our benefactors and their families and friends have long and healthy lives, all happiness, and may all their Dharma wishes be instantly fulfilled.

Translator's Preface

Those who want to accomplish their own goals and those of others must find happiness, but if you don't abandon harming others—which also means harming yourself—you can never find happiness.

Whatever you do, you do in order to be happy, but in reality negative actions create the cause for you to suffer; thus you harm both yourself and others, and there's no benefit whatsoever. The eight abandonments (of killing and so forth) explained here, ill will towards others and the ten non-virtues, which harm others either directly or indirectly, are all negative actions and bring no happiness at all, only suffering.

With respect to karma, positive actions cause happiness and negative actions cause suffering. For example, in this life you have received the body of a happy migratory being through having practiced morality in the past.

There are three ways for ordinary beings to realize the way phenomena exist. Some phenomena can be realized through true perception, some through inferential cognition (realizing the presence of fire from seeing smoke, for example), and others through dependence on valid quotations in which one has faith. Since you have neither clairvoyance nor omniscience, the only way to realize karma is to depend on the Omniscient One's quotations, in much the same way as you believe historical facts by depending on the knowledge and explanations of past and present historians.

If you harm others you might feel guilty in this life. Even if you don't feel guilty, harming others causes you to have many enemies and brings neither happiness nor relaxation to your mind; instead, it makes you insecure and fearful. This can be seen by examining the experiences of people who have done such negative actions. Cancer and AIDS, for example, are results of previous negative karma. By observing the results of non-virtuous actions you can develop a definite understanding of how worthwhile it is to abandon them. This is the foundation of all happiness.

Others don't want you to harm them; all they want is benefit and happiness, just as you don't want any harm from them, only benefit. You are completely responsible for bringing happiness to all sentient beings. By your making a vow to abandon harming them by killing them and so forth, the numberless other sentient beings stop being harmed by you and instead receive happiness. In this way you become completely responsible for the happiness of all sentient beings.

Practicing the eight-limbed Mahayana Method of Restoring and Purifying is the supreme method for avoiding harm to all sentient beings and bringing them happiness and benefit. It is easy to do and has immeasurable benefit. With this fundamental practice of morality—abstaining from harming others—you can help effect world peace.

No matter how many meetings are held in the name of world peace, there will be no benefit until people begin to abstain from harming others. Keeping the Eight Mahayana Precepts for one day, or even one hour, and thus protecting your mind from disturbing negative thoughts becomes a contribution to peace not only for the human beings of this world but also for all other sentient beings. So, while you have this precious human rebirth, it is most essential to make your life as meaningful as possible and not cheat yourself.

I have prayed that those who read this teaching, let alone who practice it, will never be reborn in the lower realms, and especially that they will generate bodhicitta and quickly attain enlightenment.

> For the sake of all mother sentient beings, may I actualize this book. May those who read it generate the wish to take the Eight Mahayana Precepts and, until they achieve enlightenment, may they always be free from rebirth in the lower realms and never be separated from qualified Mahayana teachers.

> By sentient beings' seeing this book and by the practice of the Eight Mahayana Precepts, may all epidemic diseases, cancer, AIDS, and all other sicknesses by cured; may all disputes, wars and famines stop immediately; may the rains fall at the right time and may all harvests be abundant; may sentient beings experience all enjoyments and an abundance of all that is good; may there be peace in the world; and may everyone find happiness.

> —*Lama Zopa Rinpoche, Dharamsala 1990*

1

The Benefits of Protecting the Eight Mahayana Precepts: Restoring Broken Vows and Purifying Negative Karma
by

His Holiness Trijang Dorje Chang[1]

THE SHORTCOMINGS OF DEGENERATING THE PRECEPTS

It is said in the Vinaya teaching, *Vinaya Transmission,* that even if one transgresses the great word of the Lord only a few times, one still experiences ill effects. Being non-virtuous and transgressing Buddha's teachings lead to rebirth in the animal realms, as with the naga Elapatra.

In former times, when Shakyamuni Buddha, the Destroyer, the Qualified, the One Gone Beyond, was giving a discourse, Elapatra, King of the Nagas, whose name means "having branches of the ela," transformed himself into a wheel-turning king to attend. Knowing who was sitting before him, Buddha said, "You harmed the teachings of Buddha Kashyapa [the previous Buddha]–are you now going to harm my teachings as well? Please listen to the teachings in your true form."

The next day an enormous serpent with an *eladub* tree growing out of its head came to the discourse. When the wind blew through the branches of the tree it caused intense pain deep inside the serpent's brain. The serpent was so huge that when its head had reached Buddha its tail was still leaving the village of Dorjun. Buddha's disciples were terrified and began to run away, but Buddha said, "You need not be afraid. This serpent is the very same being that appeared here yesterday in the form of a wheel-turning king." They asked Buddha what had caused the naga king to be born with such a monstrous body. Buddha explained that once, during the time of Buddha Kashyapa, the naga king had been a fully ordained monk who, while circumambulating an eladub tree, had hit his head on a branch and become angry. This disturbance weakened his precept [of abstaining from the unnecessary destruction of plants], and he lopped off the branches of the tree. This was the action that caused his present rebirth.

Reflecting on the shortcomings of breaking even this small precept, we should protect our vows properly.

THE ACTUAL BENEFITS OF PROTECTING THE PRECEPTS

The specific benefits of protecting the eight branches of the Restoring and Purifying Ordination

The benefits of abandoning the taking of life. In this life and in all future lives one's life will be long, magnificent and free from illness.

The benefits of abandoning taking that which is not given. In this and in all future lives one will have perfect enjoyments, and others will not harm them.

The benefits of abandoning the sexual act. In this life and in all future lives one will have a good body with a beautiful complexion and complete sense organs.

The benefits of abandoning lies. In this life and in all future lives one will not be cheated, and others will take heed of what one says.

The benefits of abandoning intoxicants (including alcohol, cigarettes, mind-altering drugs and any other substance that loosens voluntary reserve). In this life and in all future lives one will have stable mindfulness and awareness, clear senses and perfect wisdom.

The benefits of abandoning large and high beds and thrones. In this life and in all future lives one will receive praise and respect from others, one will have proper bedding (soft, warm, whatever is needed), and one will have vehicles and animals for traveling.

The benefits of abandoning food at improper times. In this life and in all future lives one will have abundant and perfect crops and will obtain food and drink without effort.

The benefits of abandoning perfume, ornaments, and so forth. In this life and in all future lives one's body will have a pleasant scent, color and shape and many auspicious marks.

The benefits of abandoning singing and dancing. In this life and in all future lives one will have a subdued body and mind, and one's speech will continually make the sound of Dharma.

The general benefits of protecting the eight branches of the Restoring and Purifying Ordination

The great benefit in dependence upon time. In *Victorious Concentration Sutra,* Buddha says that if with a calm mind one makes offerings of umbrellas, victory banners, light and jewel ornaments to a hundred billion buddhas for eons equal to the number of sand grains in the Ganges River, a great deal of merit is acquired. However, if, during these degenerate times when the holy Dharma, the teaching of the One Gone to Bliss, has almost ceased, one keeps just one precept for a day and a night, the merit acquired is far greater than that of giving all those offerings to an uncountable number of buddhas over such a long period.

Therefore, if the Restoring and Purifying Ordination is protected just once in one's life, the amount of merit accumulated is equal to the vastness of the sky and, as one accumulates this merit, one gradually achieves perfect happiness. By understanding this, one can see how fortunate one is to have the opportunity to take the ordination and how meaningful it is during these difficult and degenerate times. It is like finding billions of wish-fulfilling gems.

Even though one may not own one atom of a precious gem or have a single dollar, by keeping this ordination one can attain both temporary and ultimate happiness. The person who owns enough wish-fulfilling gems to fill the sky but does not keep even one branch of morality cannot attain rebirth as a human or a god, cannot practice Dharma to accomplish any of the three great purposes (higher rebirth, liberation or enlightenment), and cannot enjoy perfect helpers and enjoyments.

The great benefit in dependence upon the place. If one practices pure virtue in a pure realm for eons, the merit accumulated is not as great as that acquired by practicing virtue in an impure realm for the duration of a finger snap.

The benefit in dependence upon the nature of the precepts. In the sutras Buddha explained that if the most vicious of serpents, the great black *naga*, cannot harm those living in perfect morality, then there is no doubt that others cannot harm them.

The fully ordained monk [*gelong*] who lives within morality glows (with purity). Living in morality brings peace and happiness. Infinite benefits of morality can be described. (The best way to protect oneself from outer harm is to protect the inner ordination.) Just as a person without eyes cannot see shapes, a person without morality cannot attain liberation.

The benefit of creating the cause to meet the teachings of Maitreya Buddha. Maitreya Buddha promised that anyone who listens with devotion to the teachings of Shakyamuni Buddha and protects the

Restoring and Purifying Ordination will be born amongst his retinue as a disciple.

Therefore, if one wants to bring one's cyclic existence to an end in the future by meeting the teachings of Maitreya Buddha, then now, while one has this precious human body with its eight freedoms and ten endowments and has met Buddha's teachings and Mahayana teachers, it is extremely worthwhile to take the ordination of the Eight Mahayana Precepts and to protect these vows well.

The benefit of receiving protection from the gods. Many sutras explain that if one protects the precepts properly, the gods who are fond of virtue will protect one day and night.

The benefit of great power. Merit accumulated by one who protects the precepts is very powerful. A person living in the precepts who offers the Triple Gem a drop of butter that is only enough to cover the tip of a needle creates far greater merit than one not living in the precepts who offers the Triple Gem an ocean of butter. Merit accumulated over many eons by one not living in the Restoring and Purifying Ordination cannot be compared to the merit accumulated in just a short time by one living in the ordination.

The benefit of obtaining, without doubt, whatever one wishes. During this degenerate age, one who takes the Eight Mahayana Precepts and keeps them purely will definitely receive whatever one prays for.

The benefit of receiving the good body of a human or a god. If one protects the Eight Mahayana Precepts just once, one will attain the special bodies of gods or humans. Stories proving the benefits of such rebirths are too numerous to mention here.

The benefit of being an object for the accumulation of merit by others. One who takes ordination becomes an object for the accumulation of merit by others through becoming a (proper) object for offerings, prostrations, and so on. The higher number of precepts held by monks and nuns are the cause for others to create greater and more powerful merit by making offerings and so forth.

The benefit of simplicity. The Eight Mahayana Precepts has the advantage of being easy to take. It is said in *A Guide to the Bodhisattva's Way of Life* that if while bearing hardships of recitation over a long period, even many eons, one is distracted by other objects while reciting, the recitations will bear no fruit. To cultivate virtue through recitation there must be great concentration and no mental wandering from the beginning, through the middle to the end. Without proper concentration, all the difficulties borne during the recitation become meaningless.

On the other hand, with the Eight Mahayana Precepts one need pay attention for only the few minutes it takes to complete the ordination ceremony; afterwards, even if one's mind is distracted, the benefits of taking the precepts are not diminished. Also, there are fewer precepts than in other ordinations and they have to be kept for only one day, a very short time. For myself and others like me there is no practice easier than this. When done, it has great meaning.

The benefit of liberation and full enlightenment. Protecting the Eight Mahayana Precepts (which are also known as the Eight Fast-Day Vows) becomes the cause ultimately to achieve full enlightenment. In *Sutra Requested by Deva,* Shakyamuni Buddha said, "Goshika, by protecting the Eight Mahayana Precepts on the eighth and fifteenth days [of the month] and during the month of Buddha's Great Miraculous Deeds, one attains no less than Buddhahood."

There is no question that one will receive the body of a god as well as peerless enlightenment by taking and maintaining the precepts. Furthermore, the qualities of a buddha's holy form body, the thirty-two holy signs and the eighty holy exemplifications, are achieved by having protected the eight branches in the past. Shakyamuni Buddha, who completed the mind-training in compassion for every sentient being, would not lie and can be fully trusted—if not because of his omniscient mind, then because of his great compassion. Since we do not have the clairvoyance to see karma and all its effects, we must rely on the explanations given by Shakyamuni Buddha, the fully enlightened one, who possesses great compassion, omniscient mind and perfect power. If we cannot trust the words of such a compassionate, fully enlightened being, then who can we trust to help us to complete the inner development of our minds?

In *Sutra Requested by Kundu Sanring,* the kind and compassionate Buddha was asked, "What previous karma did you, the Destroyer, the Qualified, the One Gone Beyond, collect in order to achieve the vajra holy body, the Buddha body possessing all qualities up to the inconceivable *ushnisha* [crowning top-knot]?"

The Destroyer, the Qualified, the One Gone Beyond answered, "This is the result of having practiced in past lives the morality of abandoning killing by pacifying the mental afflictions that would cause me to shorten the lives of others."

"Why do the Buddha's hands have thousand-spoked golden wheels and long fingers with webs of light?"

"This is the benefit of having practiced in past lives the morality of abandoning taking that which is not given."

"Why does the Buddha have complete senses and a fully developed body?"

"This is the result of having practiced in past lives the morality of abandoning sexual misconduct, which is caused by mental afflictions."

"Why does the Buddha have a tongue that can cover the whole mandala face and holy speech so sweet and enchanting, like the sweet sound of Brahma?"

"This is the result of having practiced in past lives the morality of abandoning alcohol, which makes the intoxicated careless."

"Why does the Buddha have forty complete teeth, even and white, and why does he experience the highest and best tastes in food?"

"This is the result of having practiced in past lives the morality of abandoning taking food at improper times, motivated by mental afflictions."

"Why is the Buddha's body pervaded by the fragrant scent of morality?"

"This is the result of having practiced in past lives the morality of abandoning perfumes and colors [make-up], worn out of mental affliction."

"Why is the Buddha's holy body adorned with holy signs?"

"This is the result of having practiced in past lives the morality of abandoning singing, dancing and wearing ornaments out of mental affliction."

"Why does the Buddha enjoy the three seats of Dharma [lotus and sun and moon discs]?"

"This is the result of having practiced in past lives the morality of abandoning the use of large and high thrones and beds through mental affliction."

"Why does the Buddha have complete and clear senses, and why is one's enjoyment of seeing the Buddha's holy body never satiated?"

"This is the result of having practiced in past lives the morality of abandoning telling lies out of mental affliction."

"Why does the Buddha have an inconceivably high *ushnisha*?"

"This is the result of in past lives having touched the ground with the five parts of the body [the four limbs and the head] in prostration and having made offerings to Buddha, Dharma, Sangha, the guru, the leader of the disciples [preceptor] and the abbot."

Infinite benefits could be mentioned, but only a few are described here, most of which are specifically mentioned in the benefits of the near-abiding *pratimoksha* [self-liberation] vows. The eight precepts of the one-day Mahayana Restoring and Purifying Ordination are similar to these pratimoksha vows, so one can rest assured that the benefits are also similar.

THE METHOD OF COMMITMENT

The eight branches of the near-abiding pratimoksha vows and the eight branches of the Mahayana Restoring and Purifying vows are the same in their observation of the eight abandonments, but vastly different in other ways.

The first and foremost difference is the source of the ordinations. The practice of the near-abiding pratimoksha method comes from *Sutra of Dam-say Ne-jo*, whereas the Mahayana Restoring and Purifying Ordination is taken from the tantric text *Don-zhag Zhi-moi*.

The second difference is that the near-abiding pratimoksha vows cannot be taken by those with the ordination of renunciation [*rab-jung*], but the Mahayana Restoring and Purifying Ordination may be taken even by a fully ordained vajra master.

The third difference is in the motivation for taking the ordinations. The near-abiding pratimoksha ordination is taken in dependence upon the attitude of seeking the sorrowless state for oneself alone, while the Mahayana Restoring and Purifying Ordination is taken with the attitude of definitely achieving enlightenment for the sake of others.

The fourth difference is in the method of taking the ordinations. The preparation for taking the near-abiding pratimoksha ordination is to request attention and go for refuge, as in the sutra *Dam-say Ne-jo*. The preparation for the Mahayana Restoring and Purifying Ordination, as explained in the tantric text *Don-zhag Zhi-moi,* is first to request the attention of all the buddhas and bodhisattvas of the ten directions and then to promise three times to protect the precepts by following the example of the previous Victorious Ones.

The final difference is in the result achieved. The holder of the near-abiding pratimoksha vows will achieve, according to his or her motivation, the sorrowless state of both the lower and greater vehicles, whereas the holder of the Mahayana Restoring and Purifying Ordination who does not degenerate the vows will definitely achieve full enlightenment.

2

The Way in Which the Mahayana Ordination Is Taken
by

His Holiness Trijang Dorje Chang[2]

Waking early, wash and refresh yourself properly and then set up an altar for the Triple Gem in a clean and beautiful place. The offerings should be as plentiful and delightful as you can make them. The precepts are taken in the early hours just before dawn, when the lines on the palm of your [outstretched] hand are just visible.

Contemplate the shortcomings of ordinary sufferings and their true cause in relation to yourself. Remember the pitiful state of all mother sentient beings throughout infinite space, and from the depths of your heart think that you, the fortunate one, are able to seek and attain enlightenment. Now, in the presence of the holy objects and with great respect and devotion, take the Mahayana ordination.

Recite the following prayers (See *The Eight Mahayana Precepts: The Complete Practice*, pp 12–21):

Refuge and generating bodhicitta (3x)
Purifying the place
Offering prayer
Offering cloud mantra (3x)
The power of truth
Invocation

After the invocation, visualize that your infinitely kind root guru Avalokiteshvara, surrounded by the buddhas and bodhisattvas of the ten directions, actually appears in space before you.

Recite the seven-limb prayer.
Offer a mandala in order to receive the ordination.
Make three prostrations reciting the OM NAMO MANJUSHRIYE mantra with each one.

Then, kneeling on your right knee, with head and shoulders bowed and your hands together in prostration, generate the following motivation:

"Even though I and all sentient beings, who equal the extent of infinite space, have experienced countless forms of suffering from beginningless time until now (such as the general sufferings of cyclic existence and, particularly, the sufferings of the three lower realms), still I am unable to generate a single thought of aversion or frustration at this existence. Instead, because of the power of misguided habits such as grasping at suffering as happiness and grasping at that which is selfless as having a self, I am under the control of the afflictions and their actions (karma), and once again I will have to experience and endure without choice the sufferings of cyclic existence and the three lower realms, even more extensively and abundantly than before.

"If I were to really consider this situation it would definitely bring pain to my heart, anger and upset. However, even Shakyamuni Buddha and all the other buddhas of the past were not always buddhas. Like me, they once lived in cyclic existence and then, through the kindness of just one virtuous friend they had met, they generated the thought to definitely emerge from cyclic existence and the awakening mind of loving concern for each and every sentient being. Then, by taking this Mahayana ordination and protecting the precepts purely and by training in the path, they attained enlightenment.

"Similarly, having met the Mahayana teachings through the kindness of my virtuous teacher, I too will generate the altruistic aspiration to attain enlightenment and train in the path. In this way I shall definitely attain the state of enlightenment—this (thought) is the close friend from which I must never be separated, on the basis, on the path and at the result.

"Like a wish-fulfilling jewel, mother sentient beings, who equal the extent of infinite space, are the source of all the collections of excellence in this and future lives. Since beginningless time, all mother sentient beings have held me dear and are still doing so, and they will continue to do so until the end of cyclic existence. If I renounce them, and in earnest devotion seek the means for my happiness alone, this would not only be unwise and foolish but would also make me not the slightest bit different from an animal. Therefore, for the benefit of all sentient beings, who equal the extent of infinite space, I must attain the precious state of perfect and fully completed enlightenment. For this purpose, before all buddhas and bodhisattvas as my witness, I shall take the Mahayana precepts and protect them well until sunrise tomorrow."

TAKING THE PRECEPTS

The precepts should be taken with such great commitment that tears come to your eyes and your hair stands on end.

Visualize Guru Avalokiteshvara before you and repeat the prayer for taking the precepts three times.

On completing the third recitation, think that you have received the vows in your continuum and rejoice.

Then regenerate the thought of bodhicitta, the altruistic aspiration to attain enlightenment for the sake of all sentient beings, by thinking, "Just as the previous arhats abandoned all faulty behavior of body and speech, such as killing and so forth, and mentally turned away from them, similarly, I too shall properly practice the trainings by avoiding those faulty behaviors for one day for the welfare of all sentient beings."

Recite the commitment prayer to keep the precepts.

Recite the mantra of pure morality twenty-one times.

Finally, recite the prayer to keep one's morality pure, make three prostrations and dedicate the merits.

In this way, the practice is adorned by prayer and dedication and has been described for those taking the Mahayana precepts by themselves. If you are taking the precepts before a master, offer him a mandala. The master himself will have first taken the precepts (that morning) alone and is required to explain well the thoughts and visualizations of the practice, from beginning to end. In the prayer for taking the precepts, the line that says, "Master, please pay attention to me," must be included. The prayer for taking the precepts and the prayer of the precepts are both repeated after the master. The procedure for taking the precepts and the recitations should all be done in accordance with the practices of the lineage.

Refuge

La ma sang gyä la ma chhö
De zhin la ma ge dün te
Kün gyi je po la ma te
La ma nam la kyab su chhi   (3x)

Generating bodhicitta

Dag dang zhän dön drub lä du
Dag gi jang chhub sem kye do   (3x)

Purifying the place

Tham chä du ni sa zhi dag
Seg ma la sog me pa dang
Lag thil tar nyam bäiduryäi
Rang zhin jam por nä gyur chig

Offering prayer

Lha dang mi yi chhö päi dzä
Ngö su sham dang yi kyi trül
Kün zang chhö trin la na me
Nam khäi kham kün khyab gyur chig

Offering cloud mantra

OM NAMO BHAGAVATE VAJRA SARA PRAMARDANE /
TATHAGATAYA / ARHATE SAMYAKSAM BUDDHAYA /
TADYATHA / OM VAJRE VAJRE / MAHA VAJRE / MAHA TEJA VAJRE /
MAHA VIDYA VAJRE / MAHA BODHICHITTA VAJRE / MAHA BODHI
MÄNDO PASAM KRAMANA VAJRE / SARVA KARMA AVARANA VISHO
DHANA VAJRE SVAHA   (3x)

The power of truth

Kön chhog sum gyi den pa dang
Sang gyä dang jang chhub sem pa tham chä kyi jin gyi lab dang
Tshog nyi yong su dzog päi nga thang chhen po dang

3

The Eight Mahayana Precepts:
The Complete Practice[3]

Refuge
The guru is Buddha; the guru is Dharma;
The guru is Sangha also.
The guru is the creator of all (happiness);
To all gurus I go for refuge.   (3x)

Generating bodhicitta
To accomplish my own and others' aims,
I generate the mind seeking enlightenment.   (3x)

Purifying the place
Everywhere may the ground be pure,
Free of the roughness of pebbles and so forth.
May it be in the nature of lapis lazuli
And as smooth as the palm of one's hand.

Offering prayer
May human and divine offerings,
Actually arranged and mentally created,
Clouds of finest Samantabhadra offerings,
Fill the entire space.

Offering cloud mantra
OM NAMO BHAGAVATE VAJRA SARA PRAMARDANE /
TATHAGATAYA / ARHATE SAMYAKSAM BUDDHAYA /
TADYATHA / OM VAJRE VAJRE / MAHA VAJRE / MAHA TEJA VAJRE /
MAHA VIDYA VAJRE / MAHA BODHICHITTA VAJRE / MAHA BODHI
MÄNDO PASAM KRAMANA VAJRE / SARVA KARMA AVARANA VISHO
DHANA VAJRE SVAHA   (3x)

The power of truth
By the power of truth of the Three Jewels,
Of the blessings of all the buddhas and bodhisattvas,
By the power of the great might of the completed two collections,

Chhö kyi ying nam par dag ching sam gyi mi khyab päi tob kyi de
zhin nyi du gyur chig

Invocation
Ma lü sem chän kün gyi gön gyur ching
Dü de pung chä mi zä jom dzä lha
Ngö nam ma lü yang dag khyen gyur päi
Chom dän khor chä nä dir sheg su söl

Seven-limb prayer
Go sum gü päi go nä chhag tshäl lo
Ngö sham yi trül chhö trin ma lü bül
Thog me nä sag dig tung tham chä shag
Kye phag ge wa nam la je yi rang
Khor wa ma tong bar du leg zhug nä
Dro la chhö kyi khor lo kor wa dang
Dag zhän ge nam jang chhub chhen por ngo

Extensive mandala offering
OM vajra bhumi AH HUM / wang chhen ser gyi sa zhi / OM vajra rekhe
AH HUM / chhi chag ri khor yug gi kor wäi ü su

rii gyäl po ri rab / shar lü phag po / lho dzam bu ling / nub ba lang
chö / jang dra mi nyän / lü dang lü phag / nga yab dang nga yab
zhän / yo dän dang lam chhog dro / dra mi nyän dang dra mi nyän
gyi da

rin po chhei ri wo / pag sam gyi shing / dö jöi ba / ma mö pa'i lo tog
/ khor lo rin po chhe / nor bu rin po chhe / tsün mo rin po chhe /
lön po rin po chhe / lang po rin po chhe / ta chog rin po chhe / mag pön
rin po chhe / ter chen pö'i bum pa

geg ma / threng wa ma / lu ma / gar ma / me tog ma / dug pö ma /
nang säl ma / dri chhab ma / nyi ma / da wa / rin po chhei dug

chhog lä nam par gyäl wäi gyän tshän / ü su lha dang mii yi päl jor
phün sum tshog pa ma tshang wa me pa tsang zhing yi du ong wa

And of the completely pure, inconceivable sphere of reality,
May all these offerings become just so.

Invocation
Protector of all beings without exception;
Divine destroyer of the intractable legions of Mara;
Perfect knower of all things:
Bhagavan and retinue, please come here.

Seven-limb prayer
Reverently, I prostrate with my body, speech, and mind;
I present clouds of every type of offering, actual and imagined;
I declare all my negative actions accumulated since beginningless
    time
And rejoice in the merit of all holy and ordinary beings.
Please, remain until the end of cyclic existence
And turn the wheel of Dharma for living beings.
I dedicate my own merits and those of all others to the great
    enlightenment.

Extensive mandala offering
OM vajra ground AH HUM, mighty golden ground. OM vajra fence
AH HUM.

Outside it is encircled by the surrounding wall, in the center of
which are Sumeru, King of Mountains; the eastern continent,
Videha (Tall-body Land), the southern, Jambudvipa (Rose-apple
Land), the western, Godaniya (Cattle-gift Land), the northern,
Kuru; [the eastern minor continents] Deha and Videha, [the south-
ern], Camara and Apara-camara (Chowrie-land and western
Chowrie-land), [the western], Satha and Uttara-mantrin (Lands of
the Deceitful and the Skilled in Mantra), [and the northern], Kuru
and Kaurava. [In the four continents are:] [E] the precious moun-
tain, [S] the wish-granting tree, [W] the wish-fulfilling cow, [N] the
unploughed harvest.

[On the first level are:] The precious wheel, the precious jewel, the
precious queen, the precious minister, the precious elephant, the
precious horse, the precious general, and the great treasure vase.

[On the second level, the eight goddesses:] Lady of grace, lady of

di dag drin chen tsa wa dang gyü par che päi päl dän la ma dam pa
nam dang / khyä par dü yang la ma lo zang thub wang dor je chang
/ chen pö lha tshog kor dang chä päi nam la zhing kham ül war gyi
wo

thug je dro wäi dön du zhe su söl / zhe ne kyang dag sog dro wa ma
gyur nam khäi tha dang nyam päi sem chen tham chä la thug tse wa
chhen pö go nä jin gyi lab tu söl

Brief mandala offering
Sa zhi pö kyi jug shing me tog tram
Ri rab ling zhi nyi dä gyän pa di
Sang gyä zhing du mig te ül wa yi
Dro kün nam dag zhing la chö par shog

Dag gi chhag dang mong sum kye wäi yül
Dra nyen bar sum lü dang long chö chä
Phang pa me par bül gyi leg zhe nä
Dug sum rang sar dröl war jin gyi lob

IDAM GURU RATNA MANDALAKAM NIRYATAYAMI

Prostration mantra
OM NAMO MANJUSHRIYE NAMAH SUSHRIYE NAMA UTTAMA SHRIYE
SVAHA   (3x)

Taking the Eight Mahayana Precepts
Chhog chu na zhug päi sang gyä dang / jang chhub sem pa tham
chä dag la gong su söl / lob pön gong su söl / ji tar ngön gyi de zhin
sheg pa dra chom pa yang dag par dzog päi sang gyä ta chang she ta

garlands, lady of song, lady of dance, lady of flowers, lady of incense, lady of lamps, lady of perfume. [On the third level:] The sun and the moon; the precious parasol, and the banner of victory in all quarters.

In the center, the most perfect riches of gods and human beings, with nothing missing, pure and delightful.

To my glorious, holy and most kind root and lineage gurus, and in particular to the deity host of Lama Tsong Khapa, King of Sages, Maha-Vajradhara, and their divine retinue, I shall offer these as a buddha-field.

Please accept them with compassion for the sake of migrating beings. Having accepted them, to me and all migrating mother sentient beings as far as the limits of space, out of your great compassion, please grant your inspiration!

Brief mandala offering
This ground, anointed with perfume, strewn with flowers,
Adorned with Mount Meru, four continents, the sun and the moon:
I imagine this as a buddha-field and offer it.
May all living beings enjoy this pure land!

The objects of my attachment, aversion and ignorance—
Friends, enemies, strangers—and my body, wealth, and enjoyments;
Without any sense of loss I offer this collection.
Please accept it with pleasure and bless me with freedom from the
    three poisons.

IDAM GURU RATNA MANDALAKAM NIRYATAYAMI

Prostration mantra
OM NAMO MANJUSHRIYE NAMAH SUSHRIYE NAMA UTTAMA SHRIYE SVAHA   (3x)

Taking the Eight Mahayana Precepts
All buddhas and bodhisattvas dwelling in the ten directions, please pay attention to me. Just as the previous tathagatas, foe destroyers, perfectly completed buddhas who, like the divine wise horse and the

wu / lang po chhen po / ja wa jä shing je pa jä pa / khur bor wa / rang
gi dön je su thob pa / si par kün tu jor wa yong su zä pa / yang dag päi
ka / leg par nam par dröl wäi thug / leg par nam par dröl wäi she rab
chän / de dag gi / sem chän tham chä kyi dön gyi chhir dang / phän
par ja wäi chhir dang / dröl war ja wäi chhir dang / mu ge me par
ja wäi chhir dang / nä me par ja wäi chhir dang / jang chhub kyi
chhog kyi chhö nam yong su dzog par ja wäi chhir dang / la na me
pa yang dag par dzog päi jang chhub nge par tog par ja wäi chhir so
jong yang dag par dzä pa de zhin du dag [*ming*] (*say your name*) di
zhe gyi wä kyang / dü di nä zung te ji si sang nyi ma ma shar gyi
bar du / sem chän tham chä kyi dön gyi chhir dang / phän par ja
wäi chhir dang / dröl war ja wäi chhir dang / mu ge me par ja wäi
chhir dang / nä me par ja wäi chhir dang / jang chhub kyi chhog
kyi chhö nam yong su dzog par ja wäi chhir dang / la na me pa yang
dag par dzog päi jang chhub nge par tog par ja wäi chhir so jong
yang dag par lang war gyi o   (3x)

[Then the guru will say, "tab yin-no," upon which you say, "leg-so."]

*Upon completing the third recitation, think that you have received the
vows in your continuum in the form of light and rejoice. Then regenerate the thought of bodhicitta, the altruistic aspiration to attain
enlightenment for the sake of all sentient beings, by thinking:*

Deng nä sog chö mi ja zhing
Zhän gyi nor yang lang mi ja
Thrig päi chhö kyang mi chö ching
Dzün gyi tshig kyang mi ma o

The commitment prayer to keep the precepts
Kyön ni mang po nyer ten päi
Chhang ni yong su pang war ja
Thri tän chhe tho mi ja zhing
De zhin dü ma yin päi zä
Dri dang threng wa gyän dang ni
Gar dang lu sog pang war ja
Ji tar dra chom tag tu ni
Sog chö la sog mi je tar

great elephant, did what had to be done, performed actions, laid down the burden, subsequently attained their own welfare, completely exhausted the fetters to existence, and had perfect speech, well-liberated minds, and well-liberated wisdom, for the welfare of all sentient beings, in order to benefit, in order to liberate, in order to eliminate famine, in order to eliminate sickness, in order to fully complete the practices harmonious with enlightenment, and in order to definitely actualize the unsurpassed result of perfect, complete enlightenment, perfectly performed the Restoring and Purifying Ordination; similarly, also I, who am called [*say your name*], from this time until sunrise tomorrow, for the welfare of all sentient beings, in order to benefit, in order to liberate, in order to eliminate famine, in order to eliminate sickness, in order to fully complete the practices harmonious with enlightenment, and in order to definitely actualize the unsurpassed result of perfect, complete enlightenment, shall perfectly undertake the Restoring and Purifying Ordination.   (3x)

[*Then the guru will say, "This is the method," upon which you say, "Excellent."*]

Upon completing the third recitation, think that you have received the vows in your continuum in the form of light and rejoice. Then regenerate the thought of bodhicitta, the altruistic aspiration to attain enlightenment for the sake of all sentient beings, by thinking:

Just as the foe destroyers of the past have abandoned all misconduct of body, speech and mind, such as taking the lives of others, so shall I, for the sake of all beings, abandon for one day these wrong actions and devote myself to the pure practice of the training.

The commitment prayer to keep the precepts
From now on I shall not kill, steal others' possessions,
Engage in sexual activity, or speak false words.
I shall avoid intoxicants, from which many mistakes arise.
I shall not sit on large, high or expensive beds.
I shall not eat food at the wrong times.
I shall avoid singing, dancing and playing music,
And I shall not wear perfumes, garlands or ornaments.

The mantra of pure morality
OM AMOGHA SHILA SAMBHARA / BHARA BHARA / MAHA SHUDDHA
SATTVA PADMA BIBHUSHITA BHUDZA / DHARA DHARA / SAMANTA /
AVALOKITE HUM PHAT SVAHA   (21x)

Prayer to keep pure morality
Thrim kyi tshül thrim kyön me ching
Tshül thrim nam par dag dang dän
Lom sem me päi tshül thrim kyi
Tshül thrim pha röl chhin dzog shog

Make three prostrations.

Dedication prayers
Jang chhub sem chhog rin po chhe
Ma kye pa nam kye gyur chig
Kye wa nyam pa me pa yang
Gong nä gong du phel war shog

Ge wa di yi kye wo kün
Sö nam ye she tsog sag shing
Sö nam ye she lä jung wäi
Dam pa nyi yi tob par shog

Jam päl pa wö ji tar khyen pa dang
Kün tu zang po de yang de zhin te
De dag kün gyi je su dag lob chhir
Ge wa di dag tham chä rab tu ngo

Dü sum sheg päi gyäl wa tham chä kyi
Ngo wa gang la chhog tu ngag pa de
Dag gi ge wäi tsa wa di kün kyang
Zang po chö chhir rab tu ngo war gyi

Just as the arhats have avoided wrong actions, such as taking the
  lives of others,
So shall I avoid wrong actions such as taking the lives of others.
May I quickly attain enlightenment,
And may the living beings who are experiencing the various sufferings
Be released from the ocean of cyclic existence.

The mantra of pure morality

OM AMOGHA SHILA SAMBHARA / BHARA BHARA / MAHA SHUDDHA
SATTVA PADMA BIBHUSHITA BHUDZA / DHARA DHARA / SAMANTA /
AVALOKITE HUM PHAT SVAHA   (21x)

Prayer to keep pure morality

May I maintain faultless morality of the rules
And immaculate morality.
May I complete the perfection of moral conduct
By keeping morality purely and untainted by pride.

Make three prostrations.

Dedication prayers

May the supreme jewel bodhicitta
That has not arisen, arise and grow;
And may that which has arisen not diminish
But increase more and more.

Due to these virtues may all beings
Complete the collections of merit and wisdom
And attain the two holy bodies
That arise from merit and wisdom.

Just as the brave Manjushri and Samantabhadra, too,
Realized things as they are,
I, too, dedicate all these merits in the best way,
That I may follow their perfect example.

I dedicate all these roots of virtue
With the dedication praised as the best
By the victorious ones thus gone of the three times,
So I might perform good works.

4

Taking the Mahayana Restoring and Purifying Ordination

by

His Holiness Trijang Dorje Chang[4]

EXPLANATION OF THE ORDINATION PRAYER
(See pp. 17–19)

Just as the previous tathagatas. The previous buddhas, those who have gone beyond, (placed the mind in meditative equipoise) with transcendental wisdom similar to the reality of all existence, suchness and the sphere of emptiness. Another meaning of the word *tathagata* is found in the text *Expressing the Names of Manjugosha*: "As the Buddha speaks, thus he acts," which means just as the sentient beings, who are the object to be subdued, were shown practice and abandonment (the path), similarly in the past the Buddha himself entered that path and practiced until he reached the state of Buddhahood.

Foe destroyers (or *arhats*) refers to those who have destroyed without remainder all four gross and subtle hindrances (*maras*).

Perfectly completed buddhas refers to those who have completed purely all the qualities of realization and abandonment without exception; who are purified of the darkness of ignorance, which constantly disturbs with the subtle imprints of the mistakes of the hallucinated dualistic view; and who have developed the wisdom that is able to perceive all objects of knowledge of the two truths: the way things exist (the absolute truth) and how many there are (conventional truth).

Like the divine wise horse refers to the (wise) horse that is fit to be ridden by a wheel-turning king and follows a pleasant path without danger, protecting its rider. Such a horse carries its rider to a place of happiness, without disturbance. Likewise, the Buddha takes upon himself indefatigably the responsibility of working for others; that is, leading sentient beings to liberation and omniscient mind by not disturbing the three doors with mistakes of the vices.

The great elephant is an elephant that can carry a load no ordinary horse or elephant can. Similarly, the Great Compassionate One carries a load that cannot be carried by Hearers (*shravaka*) or Solitary Realizers (*pratyekabuddha*)—the constant responsibility to accomplish for all sentient beings their unsurpassable benefit and happiness without even being asked (by them to do so).

Did what had to be done means went to the limit of abandonment (of one's own work).

Performed actions means voluntarily took the responsibility of working for others in whatever way was necessary to subdue their minds.

Laid down the burden. The Buddha's mental continuum left the burden of the defiled receiver aggregates born from karma and afflictions.

Subsequently attained their own welfare. Having accomplished the works for others—the deeds of the Sons of the Victors (bodhisattvas)—they found the result, the great sorrowless state.

Completely exhausted the fetters to existence. Having exhausted the dependent arising of all arisings (all suffering comes from delusion and karma), which includes the disturbing thoughts and karma that produce their own result, true suffering.

Had perfect speech. The Buddha gives infallible advice, showing the virtuous Dharma at the beginning, in the middle and at the end. The Buddha's teaching does not deceive.

Well-liberated minds. The holy mind is liberated from the bondage of samsara, where the delusions disturb one all the time.

Well-liberated wisdom is the wisdom that is not only liberated from the obscurations of the disturbing thoughts but also well liberated from the obscurations to knowledge, thereby possessing the all-knowing transcendental wisdom.

For the welfare of all sentient beings means having given up working for oneself.

In order to benefit means to bring all sentient beings temporarily to higher rebirths.

In order to liberate means to lead them ultimately to definite goodness (liberation and enlightenment).

In order to eliminate famine refers to eliminating the poverty of not having Dharma and material needs.

In order to eliminate sickness refers to the sicknesses of body and mind and to the chronic diseases of the three poisons (anger, attachment and ignorance).

In order to fully complete the practices harmonious with enlightenment refers to the four close contemplations and so on.

And in order to definitely actualize the unsurpassed result of perfect, complete enlightenment refers to the attainment of enlightenment, with the result abandonment and the completion of all realizations.

Perfectly performed the Restoring and Purifying Ordination means the Eight Mahayana Precepts.

Similarly, also I, who am called (say your name), from this time until tomorrow sunrise, for the welfare of all sentient beings, in order to benefit, in order to liberate... and so forth means thus, for the sake of sentient beings, to benefit and liberate them, from this time until sunrise tomorrow I shall also correctly take and protect the eight-limbed ordination, which restores the Mahayana root of virtue and purifies negative karma (non-virtue). With this attitude, recite the prayer verbally.

Prayer of the precepts

With the thought of protecting the precepts, the commitment prayer should now be recited once. (See pp. 19–20)

The second part of the commitment prayer concerns the meaning of and the need for taking the precepts.

"In order to benefit sentient beings, to liberate them and so forth, from now until tomorrow sunrise I shall restore the Mahayana roots of virtue and purify all non-virtue by also taking the eight-branched ordination." Thinking in this way, recite the prayer.

Explanation of the eight branches

Recitation of the commitment prayer is followed by the method of protecting the precepts. It is not sufficient merely to receive the precepts; one must protect them from becoming undermined by recognizing the eight abandonments and observing them purely. What are these eight? They are the abandonments of the four root and the four branch vows.

The four root vows

The first root vow is to abandon killing: *From now on I shall not kill.* The basis of killing is another sentient being. Recognition of the object is the thought that identifies the object. The motivation is the intention to kill, motivated by one of the three poisons. The action completes the wish to kill by means of poison, weapon, mantra and so forth. Completion comes when the other sentient being dies before oneself. "I shall not kill" means making the commitment not to take the life of a single sentient being, from a human down to the smallest insect, from now until sunrise tomorrow.

The second root vow is to abandon taking that which is not given: *(I shall not) take others' possessions.* The basis is something that is claimed by another to be his or her own. Recognition is the thought that identifies the object. One of the three afflictions gives rise to the motivation, which is the wish to take the object, even though it has not been given. The action is performed by means of force, stealth or deceit. The completion of the action is the satisfaction that one has obtained the object. "I shall not take" means making a commitment not to take wealth or possessions that have not been given, from the most valuable to the most insignificant, such as a needle and thread, as long as the object is claimed by another to be his or her own.

The third root vow is to avoid sexual activity: *(I shall not) engage in sexual activity.* The basis of sexual misconduct is improper objects (such as one's parents), wrong organs (such as the oral or anal orifices), or women who are pregnant or observing precepts. Also included is sexual activity near holy objects, such as the guru or the Triple Gem. Recognition is the identification of the sexual object. The motivation is the intention to perform the sexual act, and comes from the afflictions, the three poisonous minds. The action is making the effort to engage in the sexual act. The completion is when the sexual organs meet and pleasure is experienced. "I shall not engage in sexual acitivity" means making the commitment not to engage in the sexual act of union of the male and female organs, or any other similar action.

The fourth root vow is to abandon lying: *(I shall not) speak false words.* The basis for telling a lie can be saying that one has seen something when one has not, heard something when one has not, remembered something when one has not, or doubted something when one has not. Or, it can be saying that one has not seen, heard, remembered or doubted something when in fact one has. The motivating affliction can be any one of the three poisons. The motivation is the wish to speak words that deceive. The action can be telling a lie oneself, getting another to lie for one, or even deceiving without actually speaking, for example, merely nodding one's head or making some other facial or physical gesture. Completion is when another person understands the (false) meaning of the action. "I shall not speak false words" means making the commitment not to lie, from the most serious way, such as lying about one's spiritual realizations, to the most simple way, or even as a joke.

The four branch vows

The first branch vow is: *I shall avoid intoxicants, from which many faults arise.* Intoxicants, such as beer, wine and so forth, are mixtures of several ingredients. Their use can unbalance the mind and definitely create the conditions for many non-virtuous harms and mistakes to arise, either quickly or gradually, depending upon one's mind. In general, ordained people are not allowed to drink even a drop of any intoxicant and, during a Mahayana ordination such as this, even lay people must abstain completely from taking intoxicants.

The second branch vow is: *I shall not sit on large, high or expensive beds.* This also refers to large thrones made of gold, silver, sandalwood, medicinal woods, precious jewels and so forth, and one must avoid seats made of glossy silk and tiger or lion skins as well.

The third branch vow is: *I shall not eat food at the wrong times.* In general, ordained people should take food at the proper time, which for them is between sunrise and noon. Upon taking the Eight Mahayana Precepts, one must avoid black foods, such as meat, eggs, garlic and onions, and eat food of the three white substances before noon, in one sitting, and not get up to take a second helping. One must then abandon eating food at the wrong time—from noon that day until sunrise the next.

The fourth branch vow is: *I shall avoid singing, dancing and playing music, and I shall not wear perfumes, garlands or ornaments.* One should not use, out of attachment, scents of incense and flowers, such as jasmine, saffron, crocus, marigold and calendula. One should not wear on the head or neck garlands of turquoise, coral, pearls or flowers. One should not wear ornaments of gold or turquoise. One should abandon dancing to rhythm, clapping one's hands or stomping one's feet for the sake of splendor or pleasure. Also to be abandoned, when done just for fun, are playing musical instruments and singing, and, for the sake of grace and charm, putting on rouge, nail polish and so forth. Massaging the body with ointments and oils should also be avoided completely.

However, there is no harm or negative karma in singing, dancing and playing musical instruments as offerings to the Triple Gem, or in sitting on a high throne to give teachings. In fact, such activities cause the accumulation of merit.

The way in which these eight branches should be protected is:

Just as the arhats have avoided wrong actions, such as taking the lives of others,
So shall I avoid wrong actions such as taking the lives of others.
May I quickly attain enlightenment,
And may the living beings who are experiencing the various sufferings
Be released from the ocean of cyclic existence.

If one wonders how one can possibly protect these vows, one should think of the previous tathagatas, who protected the precepts forever, and the shortcomings of not holding the root and branch vows of avoiding killing and so forth. One should practice these abandonments and protect them purely with all actions of body, speech and mind for the benefit of all sentient beings, thinking: "From now until sunrise tomorrow I shall abandon the eight actions of killing and so forth. By abandoning them and observing purely the eight branches, may I quickly attain unsurpassable, complete enlightenment."

And may the living beings who are experiencing the various sufferings be released from the ocean of cyclic existence refers to the fact that even after one attains full and complete enlightenment, mother sentient beings will still be living in fear, constantly tossed by the violent waves of the three sufferings (suffering of suffering, suffering of change and pervasive suffering). Think: "By myself, I shall liberate them from the four floods of birth, aging, sickness and death," and generate the altruistic Mahayana thought, aspiring to attain enlightenment for the sake of others. The importance of the need to train in the two aspirations to liberate sentient beings from cyclic existence cannot be overemphasized.

The first four vows (to avoid killing, stealing, sexual activity and lying) are the branches of practicing morality; abandoning intoxicants is the branch of practicing conscientiousness; and the remaining three (to avoid high and expensive beds and seats; singing, dancing and so forth; and taking food at improper times) are the branches of penitence.

If, having committed oneself to observing these vows, one conducts oneself carelessly, one will accumulate the shortcomings not only of not observing them, but also of telling lies. Therefore, one must protect these vows with mindfulness and awareness. If, through carelessness, the vows are degenerated, one should recite the mantra of pure morality three times to purify and restore them.

THE MANTRA OF IMMACULATE MORALITY

OM AMOGHA SHILA SAMBHARA / BHARA BHARA / MAHA SHUDDHA SATTVA PADMA BIBHUSHITA BHUDZA / DHARA DHARA / SAMANTA / AVALOKITE HUM PHAT SVAHA

This mantra is recited twenty-one times during the ordination ceremony, and its meaning is as follows:

OM	this sound adorns the beginning of most mantras
AMOGHA	meaningful
SHILA	morality
SAMBHARA	assembled
BHARA BHARA	develop, develop
MAHA	great
SHUDDHA	pure
SATTVA	mind
PADMA	lotus
BI	aspect
BHUSHITA	adorn
BHUDZA	hand
DHARA DHARA	holder, holder
SAMANTA	of all
AVALOKITE	looking with each eye (Avalokiteshvara)
HUM PHAT SVAHA	

"Assembly of morality, meaningful purified mind increase, increase, hand adorned in the aspect of the Lotus Holder, Holder of All, Avalokiteshvara."

5

Special Allowances for Taking the Precepts
by

Geshe Lamrimpa[5]

It is said in the auto-commentary to *Abhidharmakosha* that it is acceptable for people such as butchers (who do not kill at night) and prostitutes (who do not work during the day) to take the precepts for less than a day and a night. If such people take the Eight Mahayana Precepts they will have the fruits of the practice, and therefore, if the precepts are taken for just half the period and protected during that time, there is no fault; in fact, they will become very meaningful. One should try to observe the precepts for the entire period of a day and a night, but if one cannot observe them for the complete twenty-four hour period, one can observe them for half that time, or for even a half-hour. When the precepts are taken, the exact duration for which they will be observed should be stated: "from now until sunset tonight," for example.

In the teachings of Gelong Jangchub Zangpo it is said that since (the Mahayana) accepts the taking of the bodhisattva vows from now until enlightenment, this principle also applies to the Eight Mahayana Precepts, which can also be generated from now until that time.

Compendium of All Explanations (*Kun-tu Nam-sha*), composed by Gyaltseb Je, also says that the Eight Mahayana Precepts can be generated for more than twenty-four hours. He says that the assertion that the fast-day precepts are generated for only a day and a night and no longer is found in the tradition propounded by one particular Hearers' school of thought and is a mistake.

In the teachings of Maitripa, the request when the precepts are given is, "Venerable (Tib. *dzumpa*, 'firm in avoiding nonvirtue'), please pay attention to me. I, the *upasaka* [lay holder of precepts] whose name is…, until the essence of enlightenment…."

According to Kunkyen Jamyang Shepa, the method of the near-abiding eight precepts taken until enlightenment is stated in the explanations of various sutras and tantras. The Mahayana Restoring and

Purifying Ordination is definitely generated up until enlightenment because it incorporates the mind generation of bodhicitta.

Even the Lesser Vehicle tradition, which does not accept that the vow of near-abiding can last for more than one day, contains the opportunity of taking the vows for many days at one ceremony. The texts of Thubten Jhidor state that one is allowed to take the precepts for many days at a time. Even though the eight fast-day precepts are definitely a branch of the one-day approaching and abiding precepts, on occasions such as the celebration of Buddha's Great Miraculous Deeds, if the precepts are to be observed without interruption for half a month, they may be taken just once for that duration. Besides, if the ceremony of the one-day vows is recited up to fifteen times, there is no mistake in this becoming the one-day vows for as many days as the number of recitations.

The commentary to *Abhidharmakosha* says that if one is taking the fast-day precepts for a continuous period of half a month or so, it is acceptable to take them at one ceremony by reciting the prayer the same number of times as days the precepts will be observed, or else one can simply say, "I shall observe the precepts from the first day of the month until the fifteenth." Also, if one wants to take the precepts every eighth, fifteenth and thirtieth days of the month for one year, it is acceptable for one to take the vows by changing the wording to "I shall observe the precepts every eighth, fifteenth and thirtieth of each month of this year."

If the near-abiding precepts can be taken for many days at one time, there is no need to mention that the Mahayana Restoring and Purifying Ordination can be taken for as many days as one wants. Nevertheless, if one is able to take them freshly every day, there are many benefits in stabilizing memory and awareness, and the practice becomes perfect.

The question can arise, "If one degenerates one of the four root vows, is it necessary to continue to protect the other seven?" Once there were two wandering beggars, one of whom protected all his vows and, as a result, was born as a king in the human realm. The wife of the other insisted that he eat fruit in the afternoon, and he could not refuse. Due to breaking this precept he was unable to attain rebirth in the human realm, but because he observed the remaining seven precepts he was reborn as a king of the nagas. Eventually, both attained the state of a foe destroyer. Like the two beggars, one receives separately both the benefits of protecting the precepts (one keeps) and the shortcomings of not protecting the precepts (one doesn't keep).

Even if one falls short on one precept, one should protect the others as much as possible. Even if one precept, such as fasting, is broken for some reason, one should not abandon it entirely for the rest of the day—whenever possible one should still protect it. (The degenerated vow should be immediately purified and restored by reciting the purification mantra three times.)

As explained before, if one protects just one precept for even a second, one receives immeasurable benefits—benefits that are not received merely by not engaging in harmful actions (without having taken the vows). One should have the preliminary thought, "In the presence of the holy object I shall protect the vows from now until...."

In short, if one wishes not to let oneself down, even though one can protect only one precept, one should protect it. Furthermore, even if that one precept can be kept for only a brief moment, one should protect it for that time.

6

Dedication
by

His Holiness the Fourteenth Dalai Lama

Reading about the Eight Mahayana Precepts, observing them or even rejoicing when others observe such a practice creates great positive potential in our minds. In order that this [positive potential] be of greatest benefit to us and to others, it is very helpful to dedicate it following the example of the bodhisattva Shantideva.

May all beings everywhere
Plagued by sufferings of body and mind
Obtain an ocean of happiness and joy
By virtue of my merits.

May no living creature suffer,
Commit evil or ever fall ill.
May no one be afraid or belittled,
With a mind weighed down by depression.

May the blind see forms,
And the deaf hear sounds.
May those whose bodies are worn with toil
Be restored on finding repose.

May the naked find clothing,
The hungry find food;
May the thirsty find water
And delicious drinks.

May the poor find wealth,
Those weak with sorrow find joy;
May the forlorn find hope,
Constant happiness and prosperity.

May there be timely rains
And bountiful harvests;

May all medicine be effective
And wholesome prayers bear fruit.

May all who are sick and ill
Quickly be freed from their ailments.
Whatever diseases there are in the world,
May they never occur again.

May the frightened cease to be afraid
And those bound be freed;
May the powerless find power
And may people think of benefiting each other.

Notes

1. From *Collected Works*, commentary by Trusang Rinpoche. Translated by Lama Zopa Rinpoche.
2. From *The Method for Taking the Mahayana Precepts Written in a Clear Explanation as an Ascending Stair to the Mansion of Great Purification*. Translated by Venerable Thubten Dekyong.
3. From *Nyung Nä: The Means of Achievement of the Eleven-Faced Great Compassionate One, Avalokiteshvara of the (Bhikshuni) Lakshmi Tradition*, composed by Losang Kälsang Gyatso, the Seventh Dalai Lama. Compiled and translated by Lama Thubten Zopa Rinpoche and George Churinoff. Wisdom Publications, 1995.
4. From *A Whole Single Collection*. Translated by Lama Zopa Rinpoche.
5. From a teaching given in Tibet. Translated by Lama Zopa Rinpoche and Venerable Thubten Gyatso.

Acknowledgements

Chiu-Nan Lai edited the first English version of this book with Frank Brock. Venerable Thubten Detong helped with the second edit, and Venerable Thubten Gyatso with the third (in particular, with advice from Lama Zopa Rinpoche on the translation of Special Allowances for Taking the Precepts). The whole text was then edited by Nick Ribush and checked again by Lama Zopa Rinpoche. Finally, Venerable Ailsa Cameron has edited and revised the text for this edition. The complete practice (Chapter 3) has been formatted to conform with the version in *Essential Buddhist Prayers, An FPMT Prayer Book, Volume 1,* edited by Venerable Connie Miller.

The Lama Yeshe Wisdom Archive

The Lama Yeshe Wisdom Archive (LYWA) is the collected works of Lama Thubten Yeshe and Lama Thubten Zopa Rinpoche. Its spiritual director, Lama Zopa Rinpoche, founded the Archive in 1996 to make available in various ways the teachings it contains. Publication and distribution of free books of edited teachings like this is one of the ways.

Lama Yeshe and Lama Zopa Rinpoche began teaching at Kopan Monastery, Nepal, in 1970. Since then, their teachings have been recorded and transcribed. At present the LYWA contains about 7,000 cassette tapes and approximately 45,000 pages of transcribed teachings on computer disk. Many tapes, mostly teachings by Lama Zopa Rinpoche, remain to be transcribed. As Rinpoche continues to teach, the number of tapes in the Archive increases accordingly. Most of the transcripts have been neither checked nor edited.

Here at the LYWA we are making every effort to organize the transcription of that which has not yet been transcribed, to edit that which has not yet been edited, and generally to do the many other tasks detailed as follows. In all this, we need your help. Please contact us for more information:

Lama Yeshe Wisdom Archive
PO Box 356, Weston, MA 02493, USA
Telephone (781) 899-9587; fax (413) 845-9239
info@LamaYeshe.com
www.LamaYeshe.com

THE ARCHIVE TRUST

The work of the Lama Yeshe Wisdom Archive falls into two categories: archiving and dissemination.

ARCHIVING requires managing the audiotapes of teachings by Lama Yeshe and Lama Zopa Rinpoche that have already been collected, collecting tapes of teachings given but not yet sent to the ARCHIVE, and collecting tapes of Lama Zopa's on-going teachings, talks, advice and so forth as he travels the world for the benefit of all. Tapes are then catalogued and stored safely while being kept accessible for further work.

We organize the transcription of tapes, add the transcripts to the already existent database of teachings, manage this database, have transcripts checked, and make transcripts available to editors or others doing research on or practicing these teachings.

Other archiving activities include working with videotapes and photographs of the Lamas and digitizing ARCHIVE materials.

DISSEMINATION involves making the Lamas' teachings available directly or indirectly through various avenues such as books for free distribution, regular books for the trade, lightly edited transcripts, audio- and videotapes, and articles in *Mandala* and other magazines, and on our Web site. Irrespective of the method we choose, the teachings require a significant amount of work to prepare them for distribution.

This is just a summary of what we do. The ARCHIVE was established with virtually no seed funding and has developed solely through the kindness of many people, some of whom we have mentioned at the front of this book.

Our further development similarly depends upon the generosity of those who see the benefit and necessity of this work, and we would be extremely grateful for your help.

THE ARCHIVE TRUST has been established to fund the above activities and we hereby appeal to you for your kind support. If you would like to make a contribution to help us with any of the above tasks or to sponsor books for free distribution, please contact us by any of the means shown opposite.

The LAMA YESHE WISDOM ARCHIVE is a 501(c)(3) tax-deductible, non-profit corporation (ID number 04-3374479) dedicated to the welfare of all sentient beings and totally dependent upon your donations for its continued existence.

Thank you so much for your support. You may contribute by mailing a check, bank draft or money order to our Weston address; by mailing or faxing us your credit card number or by phoning it in; or by transferring funds directly to our bank:

Name of bank: Fleet
ABA routing number 011000138
Account: LYWA 546-81495
SWIFT address: FNBB US 33

THE FOUNDATION FOR THE PRESERVATION
OF THE MAHAYANA TRADITION

The Foundation for the Preservation of the Mahayana Tradition (FPMT) is an international organization of Buddhist meditation study and retreat centers, both urban and rural, monasteries, publishing houses, healing centers and other related activities founded in 1975 by Lama Thubten Yeshe and Lama Thubten Zopa Rinpoche. At present, there are more than 150 FPMT activities in twenty-eight countries worldwide.

The FPMT has been established to facilitate the study and practice of Mahayana Buddhism in general and the Tibetan Gelug tradition, founded in the fifteenth century by the great scholar, yogi and saint, Lama Je Tsong Khapa, in particular.

Every three months, the Foundation publishes a magazine, *Mandala,* from its International Office in the United States of America. To subscribe or view back issues, please go to the *Mandala* Web site, www.mandalamagazine.org, or contact:

FPMT
125B La Posta Rd., Taos, NM 87571, USA
Telephone (505) 758-7766; fax (505) 758-7765
fpmtinfo@fpmt.org
www.fpmt.org

Our Web site also offers teachings by His Holiness the Dalai Lama, Lama Yeshe, Lama Zopa Rinpoche and many other highly respected teachers in the tradition, details about the FPMT's educational programs, a complete listing of FPMT centers all over the world and in your area, and links to FPMT centers on the Web, where you will find details of their programs, and other interesting Buddhist and Tibetan home pages.

OTHER TEACHINGS OF
LAMA YESHE AND LAMA ZOPA RINPOCHE

BOOKS PUBLISHED BY WISDOM PUBLICATIONS

Wisdom Energy, by Lama Yeshe and Lama Zopa Rinpoche
Introduction to Tantra, by Lama Yeshe
Transforming Problems, by Lama Zopa Rinpoche
The Door to Satisfaction, by Lama Zopa Rinpoche
The Tantric Path of Purification, by Lama Yeshe
The Bliss of Inner Fire, by Lama Yeshe
Ultimate Healing, by Lama Zopa Rinpoche

A number of transcripts by Lama Yeshe and Lama Zopa Rinpoche
are also available. For more information about these transcripts or
the books mentioned above, see the Wisdom Publications Web site
(www.wisdompubs.org) or contact Wisdom directly at 199 Elm
Street, Somerville, MA 02144, USA, or Wisdom distributors such
as Snow Lion Publications (USA), Wisdom Books (England) or
Mandala Books (Australia).

VIDEOS OF LAMA YESHE

Available in either PAL or NTSC formats.

Introduction to Tantra: 2 tapes, US$40
The Three Principal Aspects of the Path: 2 tapes, US$40
Offering Tsok to Heruka Vajrasattva: 3 tapes, US$50

Shipping and handling extra. Available from LYWA, Mandala Books,
Wisdom Books or Meridian Trust (London). Contact LYWA for
more details or see our Web site, www.LamaYeshe.com.

What to do with Dharma teachings

THE BUDDHADHARMA IS THE TRUE SOURCE OF HAPPINESS for all sentient beings. Books like the one in your hand show you how to put the teachings into practice and integrate them into your life, whereby you get the happiness you seek. Therefore, anything containing Dharma teachings or the names of your teachers is more precious than other material objects and should be treated with respect. To avoid creating the karma of not meeting the Dharma again in future lives, please do not put books (or other holy objects) on the floor or underneath other stuff, step over or sit upon them, or use them for mundane purposes such as propping up wobbly tables. They should be kept in a clean, high place, separate from worldly writings, and wrapped in cloth when being carried around. These are but a few considerations.

Should you need to get rid of Dharma materials, they should not be thrown in the rubbish but burned in a special way. Briefly: do not incinerate such materials with other trash, but alone, and as they burn, recite the mantra OM AH HUM. As the smoke rises, visualize that it pervades all of space, carrying the essence of the Dharma to all sentient beings in the six samsaric realms, purifying their minds, alleviating their suffering, and bringing them all happiness, up to and including enlightenment. Some people might find this practice a bit unusual, but it is given according to tradition. Thank you very much.

Dedication

THROUGH THE MERIT CREATED by preparing, reading, thinking about and sharing this book with others, may all teachers of the Dharma live long and healthy lives, may the Dharma spread throughout the infinite reaches of space, and may all sentient beings quickly attain enlightenment.

In whichever realm, country, area or place this book may be, may there be no war, drought, famine, disease, injury, disharmony or unhappiness, may there be only great prosperity, may everything needed be easily obtained, and may all be guided by only perfectly qualified Dharma teachers, enjoy the happiness of Dharma, have love and compassion for all sentient beings, and only benefit and never harm each other.

LAMA THUBTEN ZOPA RINPOCHE was born in Thami, Nepal, in 1946. At the age of three he was recognized as the reincarnation of the Lawudo Lama, who had lived nearby at Lawudo, within sight of Rinpoche's Thami home. Rinpoche's own description of his early years may be found in his book, *The Door to Satisfaction* (Wisdom Publications). At the age of ten, Rinpoche went to Tibet and studied and meditated at Domo Geshe Rinpoche's monastery near Pagri, until the Chinese occupation of Tibet in 1959 forced him to forsake Tibet for the safety of Bhutan. Rinpoche then went to the Tibetan refugee camp at Buxa Duar, West Bengal, India, where he met Lama Yeshe, who became his closest teacher. The Lamas went to Nepal in 1967, and over the next few years built Kopan and Lawudo Monasteries. In 1971 Lama Zopa Rinpoche gave the first of his famous annual lam-rim retreat courses, which continue at Kopan to this day. In 1974, with Lama Yeshe, Rinpoche began traveling the world to teach and establish centers of Dharma. When Lama Yeshe passed away in 1984, Rinpoche took over as spiritual head of the FPMT, which has continued to flourish under his peerless leadership. More details of Rinpoche's life and work may be found on the FPMT Web site, www.fpmt.org. Rinpoche's other published teachings include *Wisdom Energy* (with Lama Yeshe), *Transforming Problems*, *Door to Satisfaction* and *Ultimate Healing* and a number of transcripts and practice booklets (available from Wisdom at www.wisdompubs.org).